Smithsonian National Air and Space Museum

The Story of Flight

Judith E. Rinard

Firefly Books

A FIREFLY BOOK

First Printing

Publisher Cataloging-in-Publication Data (U.S.)
Rinard, Judith E.
   The story of flight : the Smithsonian National Air and Space Museum / Judith E. Rinard. —1st ed.
[64] p. : col. photos. ; cm.
Summary: Milestones in the development of flight illustrated from the collection of the National Air and Space Museum. Includes early airplanes, war planes, space travel, international space station and future of flight.
ISBN 1-55297-642-4
ISBN 1-55297-694-7 (pbk.)
1. Flight—History. 2. Aeronautics—History. 3. Aeronautics—Flights.
I. National Air and Space Museum. II. Title.
629.1309 21   CIP   TL506.U62R56 2002

National Library of Canada Cataloguing in Publication Data
Rinard, Judith E.
   The story of flight : the Smithsonian National Air and Space Museum
ISBN 1-55297-642-4 (bound).—ISBN 1-55297-694-7 (pbk.)
1. National Air and Space Museum—Juvenile literature.
2. Aeronautics—United States—History—Juvenile literature.
3. Astronautics—United States—History—Juvenile literature.
I. Title.
TL506.U62W37 2002   629.1'074'753   C2002-900639-2

Published in Canada
in 2002 by
Firefly Books Ltd.
3680 Victoria Park Avenue
Toronto, Ontario M2H 3K1

Published in the United States
in 2002 by
Firefly Books (U.S.) Inc.
P.O. Box 1338, Ellicott Station
Buffalo, New York 14205

Produced by Charles O. Hyman, Visual Communications Inc., Washington, D.C.

Designed by Kevin R. Osborn, Research and Design, Ltd., Arlington, Virginia

Smithsonian Institution
   Patricia Graboske, Publication Director
   Clare Cuddy, Educational Programs
   Melissa A. N. Keiser, Chief Photo Archivist
   Mark Avino, Eric F. Long, Carolyn Russo; Photography

Printed and bound in Canada by Friesens, Altona, Manitoba

Cover: *The SR-71 Blackbird cruises over snow-covered mountains. This reconnaissance craft is the world's fastest airplane. It can fly from Washington, D.C. to Los Angeles, California, in just 64 minutes.*

Title Page: *A young passenger poses before boarding a Flying Tiger Line Super Constellation airliner in 1957.*

Acknowledgements:
The author is grateful to the curators and other staff at the National Air and Space Museum for their assistance in making this book possible. Special thanks to Thomas Dietz, Museum Specialist in the Aeronautics Division, and to Valerie Neal and Michael Neufeld, Curators in the Space History Division. They read the manuscript and made many helpful suggestions. Thanks also to Melissa Keiser of the Archives Division, who gathered the photographs for the book and provided invaluable historical information about them. Finally, thanks to Clare Cuddy, Manager of Educational Programs, and Patricia Graboske, Chief of Publications, for their ongoing guidance and help.

The photo editor gratefully acknowledges the assistance of her colleagues at the National Air and Space Museum, particularly Kate Igoe, Dan Hagedorn, Allan Janus, Paul Silbermann, Barbara Weitbrecht, and Patricia Williams (Archives); Alex Spencer (Aeronautics); and Phil Edwards (Smithsonian Institution Libraries).

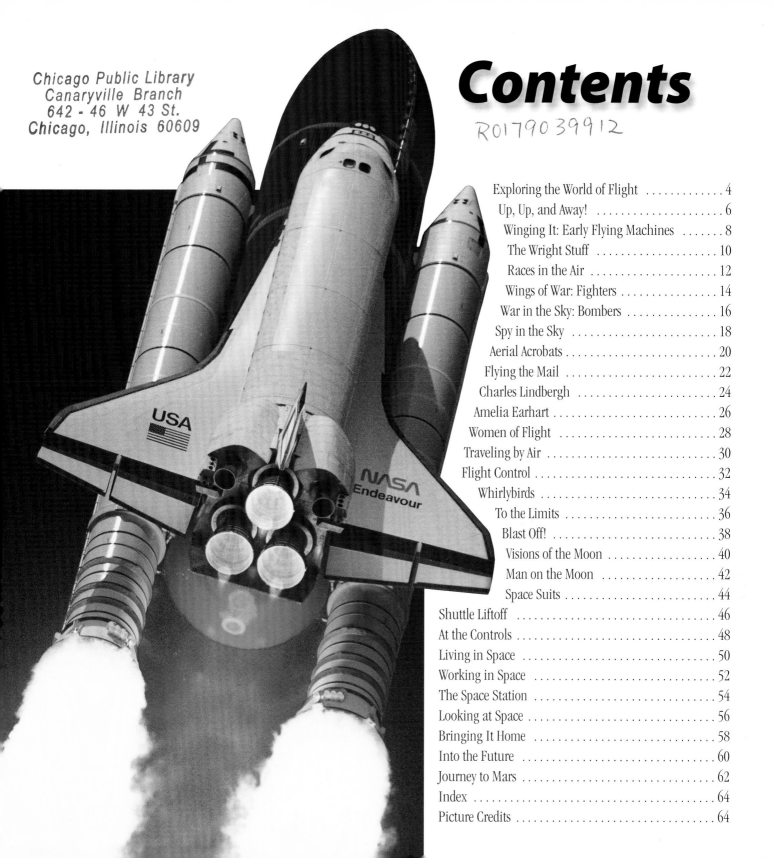

Contents

Exploring the World of Flight

Where can you walk in the door and see a collection of history's most famous airplanes and spacecraft hanging from the ceiling and displayed all around you? Here, in the Smithsonian's National Air and Space Museum in Washington, D.C. Opened in 1976, it is one of the most popular museums in the world, with over nine million visitors a year. In its displays, the museum traces the history of flight.

Today, we see jetliners, helicopters, and spacecraft zoom through the air routinely. These flying machines are a normal part of our lives. Can you imagine a world without them? Yet the very first powered airplane, flown by Wilbur and Orville Wright, took off in 1903, only a century ago! Just a few generations ago, perhaps when your great grandparents were young, it was rare and astonishing to see an airplane in the sky.

The story of flight is a story of dreams and the people who made them come true—ingenious inventors and courageous pilots. In this book, you'll stroll through the museum and travel through time. You'll see how hot-air balloons of the 1700s carried the first humans to fly, and soar with early glider pilot Otto Lilienthal.

Then, you'll meet the Wright brothers and discover how they built and flew their famous plane, the *Flyer*. You'll see it in the Milestones of Flight gallery. There, you'll also see the *Spirit of St. Louis*. In this small, silver-colored plane, Charles Lindbergh flew across the Atlantic Ocean nonstop from New York to Paris in 1927. In 1932, Amelia Earhart became the first woman to make a solo Atlantic flight. Her bright red Lockheed Vega is now in the Pioneers of Flight gallery. You'll ride with these pilots on their daring journeys.

Looking at aircraft in war, you'll see how fighter planes and bombers changed from flimsy wood-and-fabric biplanes of World War I to the sleek stealth fighter and bomber of today. You'll meet flying aces, like Germany's "Red Baron."

In other pages, you'll read about the first airmail pilots, peek inside a 1930s "flying boat," and watch daredevil pilots—barnstormers of the 1920s. You'll meet African American pioneers, Col. Benjamin Davis, who commanded the first black fighter pilots in World War II, and Bessie Coleman, a famous barnstormer. And you'll fly with test pilot Chuck Yeager in a rocket-powered plane to break the sound barrier for the first time.

In the space age, you'll discover how rockets work and join the Apollo astronauts as they step onto the moon. Then you'll blast off aboard a space shuttle, and see how astronauts live and work in space today. You'll also visit the International Space Station and learn about a future mission to Mars. In just a short time, flight has come a long way. The story is still continuing. Who knows? One day, you may create a new part of it.

Let your dreams soar!

Moonrock

At the National Air and Space Museum, you can actually touch the moon! This visitor feels a piece of lunar rock brought back by Apollo 17 astronauts in 1972. It's believed to be 4 billion years old. The only other place on Earth you can touch a lunar rock is Johnson Space Center in Houston, Texas.

Wings on Display

In the Hall of Air Transportation, you can see passenger planes of the 1920s through 1950s. Many hang from the ceiling. The museum was specially designed to hang aircraft from strong steel beams. How do the planes get in? One glass window wall opens like a huge sliding door.

Up, Up, and Away!

For centuries, people longed to fly like birds and other winged creatures. Yet it wasn't wings that first carried humans in flight. It was a giant balloon. In 1783, French brothers Joseph and Etienne Montgolfier built the first hot-air balloon. They made a huge cloth-and-paper bag. Then they attached a metal grate and built a fire in it. Hot air filled the bag and WHOOSH! It rose up, up into the sky. Why? Hot air rises because it's lighter than cooler surrounding air. The first balloon passengers were a duck, a sheep, and a rooster. Next, two noblemen—the first humans to fly—floated five miles over Paris as astonished crowds watched.

Soon, balloons filled with hydrogen, a lighter-than-air gas, also flew. In 1852, a steam engine was added, creating the first airship. Airships could be steered, unlike balloons, which drift in the wind. Today, people still fly airships and balloons. In 1999, two men even flew a balloon around the world.

Lighter than Air

People today still get a lift out of launching a balloon in France (above), where it all began. On November 21, 1783, men first flew in a balloon for 20 minutes over Paris (center). A modern airship (right) is a floating advertisement. Crew ride in a cabin, or gondola.

GOOD YEAR #1 in TIRES

Oops!

Ballooning was great fun to people of the 1800s. This 1897 music cover illustrates a "comic song" about a bridegroom. He was so caught up in ballooning he accidentally floated off and missed his own wedding.

Thrilling Ride

Hot-air ballooning is still popular today and some pilots offer rides to the public. Passengers in this pagoda-shaped balloon ride in a basket. The pilot pulls a valve. It blasts heat into the balloon from propane gas burners located under the opening.

What a Sight

Onlookers watch an airship, the first powered aircraft of the U.S. Army, fly over Virginia in 1908. Two crewmen guide the ship. Such ships used dangerously explosive hydrogen for lift. Now airships use nonflammable helium.

Winging It: Early Flying Machines

Balloons proved people could fly. Yet some inventors had not given up on wings. For ages, people had been trying to copy birds, making wings that flapped up and down. They tested them by jumping off high places and learned by hard experience that it didn't work!

In 1891, a German engineer, Otto Lilienthal, built gliders with fixed wings. He had watched birds gliding. They rode the air with their wings spread wide, not flapping. Looking like a large bird himself in his craft, Lilienthal tested the gliders by leaping from a hill. He ran, jumped into the wind, and sailed through the air. Some people watching thought he was mad. But most were thrilled to see him soar 64 feet high and glide nearly a quarter of a mile. Lilienthal could only steer his gliders by shifting his weight. In 1896, he crashed and died. Yet he had learned much about flight and his notes helped later inventors. People next tried to create a powered flying machine. They built contraptions with wings and steam engines. Some hopped off the ground. But none could really fly with a pilot in control.

Soaring like a Bird

Otto Lilienthal jumps from a hill near Berlin and soars in a glider as a crowd watches. The world's first glider pilot, he made over 2,500 glider flights. Below, a model of Lilienthal in one of his actual gliders, built of cotton fabric stretched over a willow frame, hangs in the National Air and Space Museum.

D'Equevilley's Aeroplane

Hanging in Midair

People still glide for fun. A modern hang-glider works much as Lilienthal's did, gliding on air currents. Strapped in a safety harness, the pilot dashes into the wind. The wind lifts the glider sail, or wing. The pilot can move a control bar or shift his weight to change direction.

But Will It Fly?

These early flying machines looked interesting, but none flew. The d'Equevilley multiplane (top) was modeled after a Ferris Wheel. The Gonnel uniplane (center) was a blend of plane, boat, and parachute. The Givaudan No.1 (bottom) sported two cylinder-shaped wings.

The Wright Stuff

Secret from Birds

Wilbur Wright got his idea of twisting, or warping, the Flyer's *wings for control from birds. He saw how buzzards blown by winds balanced themselves with a twist, or "torsion," of their wingtips.*

On Exhibit

The original Wright Flyer *now hangs in a place of honor in the National Air and Space Museum. A model of Orville Wright shows how he flew the plane lying down. He moved an elevator stick with his hand to go up or down and used his hips to control the wing-warping cables.*

In 1903, the first powered aircraft with a pilot in control finally flew. The plane was built by two of history's most famous inventors—Orville and Wilbur Wright. The Wright brothers grew up in Dayton, Ohio. As boys, they enjoyed building and flying kites. Their father brought them a toy helicopter, wound by a rubber band. They spent hours playing with it and watching it zoom through the air. From then on, they were fascinated by flying.

In 1892 the brothers opened a bicycle shop. They designed and built their own cycles. Soon, they decided to try building a flying machine. They read all they could on the subject. Then they experimented, first with kites, then gliders. They made a wind tunnel to test tiny wing models for the best design. Then they built a large glider with a spruce wood frame and cotton fabric wings.

The Wrights realized that to succeed, they needed to build a craft a pilot could control. They built a small front winged device called an elevator. The pilot could move it to tilt the craft's nose to go up or down. They built wire cables to warp, or twist, the plane's wings, lowering one wing tip and raising the other to balance on turns. Finally, they added their own propellers and gasoline engine. The result was a remarkable achievement—the *Flyer*. It was the world's first real airplane.

On December 17, 1903, the brothers tested their plane on the windy beach of Kitty Hawk, North Carolina. First, Wilbur tried to take off, but the plane got stuck in sand. Then Orville took a turn. As Wilbur watched, the engine sputtered to life. Suddenly the *Flyer* was flying! A witness took a photograph. The flight lasted just 12 seconds, but it changed the world. A new age of flight was born.

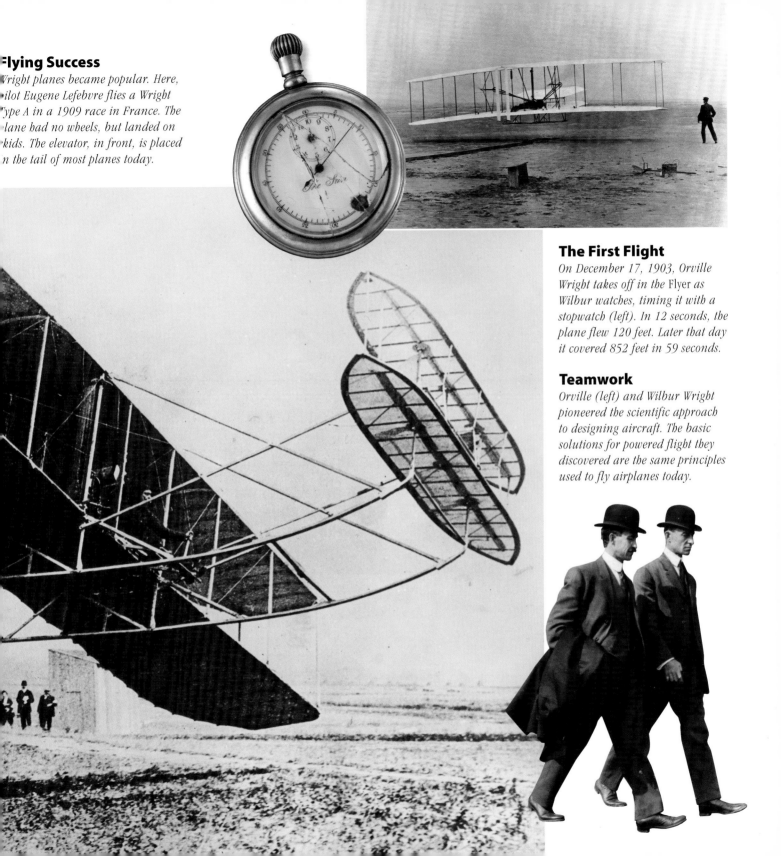

Flying Success

Wright planes became popular. Here, pilot Eugene Lefebvre flies a Wright Type A in a 1909 race in France. The plane had no wheels, but landed on skids. The elevator, in front, is placed in the tail of most planes today.

The First Flight

On December 17, 1903, Orville Wright takes off in the Flyer as Wilbur watches, timing it with a stopwatch (left). In 12 seconds, the plane flew 120 feet. Later that day it covered 852 feet in 59 seconds.

Teamwork

Orville (left) and Wilbur Wright pioneered the scientific approach to designing aircraft. The basic solutions for powered flight they discovered are the same principles used to fly airplanes today.

Races in the Air

New Design
Louis Blériot races his Blériot XII, a monoplane, or single-wing plane, at Reims, France in 1909. That year he also flew a monoplane in the first crossing of the English Channel, winning fame and a £1,000 prize.

Cub Co-pilot
Colonel Roscoe Turner, a famous racing pilot of the 1930s, poses with his pet lion, Gilmore. Turner often raced with Gilmore, who wore his own parachute.

Look Out!
A contestant crashes nose-first during a race at Reims. This was common in the early days of flight.

It didn't take long for flying to catch on. Soon it was an exciting and popular new sport. In 1909, just six years after the Wright brothers' first flight, the first world air meet was held at Reims, France. Pilots came from everywhere to test their flying skills in speed, distance, and altitude races.

As pilots competed for more prize money and fame, planes got faster. Builders tried new ideas. Instead of the biplane (double-winged plane) of the Wright brothers, some designers built monoplanes (single-winged) craft. These were trickier to fly, but speedier. Others tried triplanes (three-winged planes). By the 1930s, huge crowds were watching the U.S. National Air Races. In these races, pilots such as Roscoe Turner became sports heroes. They competed for the Thompson Trophy in speed racing and the Bendix Trophy in cross-country racing. In 1929, the first women's air race was held. Pilots also began setting new world flight records. Today, you can still see great speed and racing form at air shows and special events such as the Reno Air Races in Nevada.

Off to the Races

A poster from the museum's collection advertises the 1932 National Air Races. These annual races, begun in the 1920s, featured speed and showmanship, and thrilled thousands of fans.

Going the Distance

In record flights, Wiley Post circled the globe twice. In 1931, he flew the trip in his Lockheed Vega Winnie Mae *with a navigator in about 8 1/2 days. Here, the plane crosses the Volga River. In 1933, he flew solo.*

Built for Speed

Three F-16 fighter jets of the U.S. Air Force Thunderbirds display team streak through the sky. They perform breathtaking loops, turns, and dives while pushing to maximum speeds—over twice the speed of sound.

Wings of War: Fighters

Curse You, Red Baron!

World War I aces were heroes in early movies (above). Today, the cartoon hero Snoopy flies on a stamp. He still battles Germany's great ace, the Red Baron, Manfred von Richthofen (below). In his bright red Fokker triplane (right), the Baron chases a British Sopwith Camel.

Up until 1914, most airplanes were flown for sport or exhibition shows. But when World War I began, planes got a new job—fighting. They started out as unarmed observer craft. Yet leaders soon realized their value in combat. New planes were armed with machine guns. Pilots fought battles called dogfights. Pilots who shot down five or more planes were called "aces."

World War I fighters were fragile craft of cloth stretched over wood frames. They could fly up to 115 miles an hour. Flying the planes was difficult and dangerous. They often conked out in midair! They also went up in flames very easily, and pilots had no parachutes to bail out.

By World War II, fighters had advanced tremendously. Built of sturdy metal, they had covered cockpits, flew reliably, and reached speeds of over 400 miles an hour. Today, fighters fly twice the speed of sound to intercept enemies with computer-guided weapons.

Famous Fighter

In World War II, Colonel Benjamin Davis, shown here with a P-47D Thunderbolt, commanded the first African American fighter pilots. Called the Tuskegee Airmen, they escorted bombers. Not a single plane they protected was lost.

Invisible Shape

The Lockheed F-117A Stealth Fighter has an angled shape that deflects radar beams. This helps it fly undetected as it sneaks up on a target. Called the "Nighthawk," it specializes in night attacks.

Fighter Power

A squadron of modern F-16 fighter jets forms a wall of weapons to face an enemy. They can attack targets in the air or on the ground with cannon or missiles. The jets use advanced radar systems to locate and lock in on targets miles away.

Flying Tiger

An American pilot waves from a Curtiss P-40 Warhawk. Painted like a tiger shark, this fighter battled the Japanese in World War II. Pilots who flew these planes were called the "Flying Tigers."

War in the Sky: Bombers

At the beginning of World War I, no bomber planes existed. Fighter pilots just leaned over the sides of their planes and dropped small explosives. In 1915, Germany sent giant airships, called Zeppelins, to bomb England. The giant gas-filled ships were terrifying to see, but proved easy to shoot down. Soon, both Germany and its Allied enemies were building large bomber planes with powerful engines. They could carry bombs weighing hundreds of pounds.

During World War II bombers were bigger, more powerful, and heavily armed. They flew in large formations. Some famous U.S. bombers were the B-17 "Flying Fortress, " B-24 "Liberator," and B-29 Superfortress. Bombers dropped millions of tons of bombs in the war, on enemy cities, ships, and fuel supplies.

Today, modern bombers are highly advanced technical machines. Traveling at supersonic speed, bombers can fly thousands of miles deep inside enemy territory. They pinpoint targets with sensitive radar or laser beams. In seconds, they attack with bombs or powerful missiles.

Hand Bombing

In the earliest days of World War I, bombing was done like this: The pilot of this German Halberstadt fighter gets small bombs to drop from his cockpit. A box on his plane holds hand grenades to use.

Look Out Below!

U.S. B-29 Superfortresses, the mightiest bombers of World War II, bomb a Japanese supply station in Burma. The huge planes could carry over 20,000 pounds of bombs.

Fearsome Foe
Wearing a camouflage pattern, this Zeppelin Staaken R.IV was Germany's biggest bomber of World War I. It carried 18 huge bombs and had a wingspan of 138 feet, dwarfing a British Sopwith Camel Fighter (left).

Scoring a Hit
Diving low, U.S. Douglas Dauntless dive bombers bomb a Japanese aircraft carrier in World War II. In this battle, the bombers sank four carriers and their planes, crippling Japan's ability to wage war.

Attack!
A B-2 Stealth Bomber zeroes in on a target, escorted by F-117A Stealth Fighters. With its stealth design, the B-2 can penetrate enemy lines undetected to strike a powerful blow. Computer guided, it carries 20 tons of bombs and missiles.

Spy in the Sky

Getting a look at your enemy in war is a lot easier from high in the air. In early wars, such as the American Civil War, balloons were used to view enemy troop positions on battlefields. In World War I, pilots flying over enemy territory began taking photographs. These were the first aerial spy pictures.

During World War II, reconnaissance planes searched for enemy submarines and spied on enemy ships at sea. They also gathered information about enemy land operations.

In the 1950s, the first modern spy plane, the U-2, began flying during the Cold War between the United States and Soviet Union. It looked like a glider, with long thin wings to help it fly high, over 70,000 feet. It had a panoramic camera to take photographs and look for Soviet ballistic missiles.

A second spy plane, the Lockheed SR-71 Blackbird, was developed in the 1960s. It was the first stealth plane, designed with a flattened shape and black coating to elude radar. This amazing plane can fly higher and faster than any other aircraft today, reaching 90,000 feet and flying at three times the speed of sound. Its cameras photograph 100,000 square miles of ground an hour.

Both of these spy planes still fly today. The pictures they take help leaders cope with world conflicts. Even higher spies in the sky today are satellites. The most advanced of all satellites, they have telescopes so powerful they can see areas just a few feet wide from space!

Picture This

A World War I pilot leans out of his plane in fierce winds to snap a picture behind enemy lines. This was the start of spy plane intelligence gathering.

Airborne Observer

As a French reconnaissance pilot flies over enemy ground, he can see and photograph trenches, troops, weapons, and supplies. Maps drawn from the photographs helped leaders plan battle strategies.

Famous Spy Planes

Unmistakably different in shape, a Lockheed SR-71 (top) and U-2 fly high. A 1962 photo of Soviet missiles in Cuba (pg 18) was taken by a U-2. A satellite image of Washington, D.C. (right) was taken from a higher "eye" in space.

Cool Controls

Dials and switches line the SR-71 cockpit to fly this ultra-fast, high altitude craft. It has set world speed records, flying 2,193 miles an hour— truly faster than a speeding bullet.

Aerial Acrobats

Just Hanging Out
Dangling from a plane's wheel axle, a barnstormer waves to the crowd. The public adored such stunts and clamored for more. Fliers did airborne trapeze acts and even hung by their teeth!

Flying Fun
Two early pilots prepare to take off for a ride. Edmund Poillot (above) takes his dog for a spin in a Voisin biplane. Below, Bertram Acosta can't wait to get off the ground in his Curtiss pusher.

People have always enjoyed flying for fun—just to feel the sheer joy and freedom of soaring above the ground. And people have always enjoyed watching flying entertainment. After World War I, there were cheap military planes and many pilots who wanted to keep flying. So the pilots began traveling around the countryside, entertaining people with their flying skills. They slept in farm fields under their planes or in barns.

These fliers were called barnstormers. They performed aerobatic flying—doing dives, rolls, loops, and spins. Some also did stunt flying. They performed tricks on the wings of a flying plane. These ranged from one person doing headstands to two people setting up a net and playing tennis! Many fliers hung under the plane wings or wheels and did acrobatic routines. Others leaped from one moving plane to another or from a plane to a moving car on the ground. Still others did exciting parachute jumps. Crowds on the ground cheered with delight. After the show, barnstormers took people up for rides in exchange for money or a meal. Many pilots got early flying experience as barnstormers. One was Charles Lindbergh.

You can see modern barnstorming shows today. Many old biplanes still fly and pilots enjoy performing in them in flying air circuses.

Balancing Act

Stunt flying continues today. This modern daredevil thrills an audience by sitting on a wire chair on a Stearman biplane as it soars through the air.

On a Roll

A pair of modern barnstormers flies a double loop-the-loop maneuver in this exciting air show routine. Such moves require great timing and flying skill.

Showtime!

A vintage poster advertises a coming Air Circus. During barnstorming of the 1920s, such shows traveled from town to town. Today, many communities have old-time flying clubs and air shows.

Flying the Mail

Great Prices

Sending a letter by early airmail looks like a bargain compared to today's rates. According to this 1930s advertisement, it cost just a nickel for one ounce!

Today, we get mail delivered to our door by a mail carrier or express-mail delivery truck. We expect it to come regularly and fast, and usually it does. Yet back in the early days, it was a different story.

The first airmail service in the United States began in 1918. The U.S. Post Office bought a fleet of World War I biplanes, called Curtiss Jennies. They were rickety machines that smoked and sputtered. On the first mail flight from Washington, D.C. to New York, the pilot headed off with 140 pounds of mail—in the wrong direction!

Soon pilots were flying mail across the country in relays, like the Pony Express. They found their way by following landmarks—towns, rivers, lakes, and railroad tracks. By 1921, people were amazed at the speed airmail had reached. Seven planes carried mail from San Francisco to New York in 33 hours. It would have taken 108 hours by train.

Yet flying the mail was a hard, dangerous job. Pilots flew in planes with open cockpits in rain, snow, icy wind, and hail. They flew at night with no lights and crossed perilous mountains. The trip from New York to Chicago over the Allegheny Mountains was known as the "Graveyard Run." The reason? Between 1919 and 1920, 18 pilots died making the trip. By 1925, only nine of the 40 pilots hired by the Post Office were still alive! Private companies then took over flying mail.

Today, both the U.S. Post Office and private express companies handle mail. Many businesses rely on express mail to send important packages as quickly as possible. You can now even send mail many places overnight. How things have changed!

Speed Service

Express mail workers load packages on a plane for next-day delivery. Below, a dispatcher directs 160 planes a night to destinations nationwide. They move 3 ¹/₂ million pounds of priority and express mail every day.

Early Mail Carriers

These 1922 airmail pilots are bundled head to toe for winter. Flying in open cockpits with no heaters, they wore two layers of coats, sweaters, socks, shoes, and gloves. Below, mail is loaded from a U.S. Mail truck to a de Havilland DH-4 mail plane in 1924.

Charles Lindbergh

World Hero
Charles Lindbergh, a young mail pilot, won instant acclaim for his Atlantic flight. People all over the world admired his courage and skill. His flight gave people trust in airplanes and flying.

Charles Lindbergh was one of the most famous pilots of all time. On May 20, 1927, at age 25, he set out to win a prize of $25,000 to do what no one had done before—fly nonstop from New York to Paris, France, a distance of 3,610 miles across the wide Atlantic Ocean. And he would fly alone.

Lindbergh took off in a monoplane, the *Spirit of St. Louis*. He was so excited he hadn't slept in 24 hours. His plane was so heavy with fuel for the long flight, it barely got off the ground. To save weight, Lindbergh left his radio behind. Instead, he would rely on his few instruments and flying skill.

Soon, Lindbergh was over the ocean, miles from any help. Raging thunderstorms threw his tiny plane up and down. At times just 10 feet below, he could see the forbidding, cold waves. "It's a fierce, unfriendly sea," he wrote. "I feel naked above it…conscious of the terrific strength of the waves, of the thinness of my wings…" Imagine how frightened this young pilot must have felt! Yet he wrote, "I must go on…there's no alternative but death." Flying on through curtains of fog, Lindbergh saw enormous white pyramids—icebergs—looming in the dark sea. During the night, he flew enclosed in darkness, finding his way by only his instruments. He was so sleepy he had to fight to stay awake—and survive. At dawn, he finally spotted land. It was Ireland . He flew on and landed at last in Paris, after 33 1/2 hours in the air. Crowds rushed out to greet him. He had not slept in 57 1/2 hours. But he had won his prize, and made history.

Flying Legends
Both Lindbergh and his plane became famous. Songs were written for the pilot. His plane, painted with flags of nations he toured, hangs in the National Air and Space Museum.

Pilot's Seat
Lindbergh's tiny cockpit, behind a fuel tank, had no front window. He used a periscope or turned the plane to look out a side window.
He used his instruments to stay on course, called "flying blind."

Amelia Earhart

Lost at Sea

On July 3, 1937, Amelia Earhart disappeared while flying over the Pacific on a round-the-world trip. This song was written about her. Many experts think she ran out of fuel and crashed in the ocean.

Amelia Earhart was an adventurous young woman who became a famous pioneer of women fliers. She got her first airplane ride at a flying circus show in 1920 when she was 23. "As soon as we left the ground, I knew I myself had to fly," she wrote. Amelia loved flying for what she called just the "fun of it." Yet she also set many new records and was eager to prove women could fly as well as men.

On May 20, 1932, five years to the day after Lindbergh's flight, Amelia took off in a bright red Lockheed Vega from Newfoundland. She would become the first woman to fly solo over the Atlantic. Her trip was not easy. Her altimeter failed. Without this instrument, she couldn't tell if she was flying at a safe height above the waves. Her plane hit a violent storm. As she tried to climb above it, deadly ice formed on her wings. Suddenly, the plane plunged downward, dropping 3,000 feet! Struggling for control, Amelia finally pulled the plane up level, just in time. After nearly 15 hours, she reached Ireland and landed. Her flight made her world famous.

In 1937, Amelia set off on her biggest challenge—a trip around the world in a Lockheed Electra. As she flew with her navigator over the Pacific, her luck ran out. Her plane disappeared over the ocean. No sign of her, her navigator, or her plane was ever found. Yet Amelia had inspired other women fliers to follow their dreams. She said, "If enough of us keep trying, we'll get someplace."

Admiring Crowd
Excited fans surround Amelia's plane at Oakland, California, after her solo flight from Hawaii in 1935. Her daring feats won her acclaim and recognition. A gold medal honors her achievements.

Smiling Celebrity
During the difficult days of the Great Depression Amelia was a popular star. Here, in 1936, she poses with her Cord Cabriolet and Lockheed Electra, the plane in which she disappeared.

Famous Plane
The red Vega Amelia flew across the Atlantic in 1932 is now in the National Air and Space Museum. One of the most advanced planes of its day, it had a streamlined fuselage, or body, of wood.

Women of Flight

Throughout history, women have flown for the same reasons as men—the joy of flying, to master an exciting skill, and to achieve new goals and set new records.

The first women to take to the skies were female balloonists in the early 1800s. In 1909, Elise Deroche of France competed in the first world air meet in Reims. She scored high and became the first woman in the world to earn a pilot's license. Harriet Quimby was the first licensed American woman pilot. In 1911 she joined a flying troupe and drew crowds of thousands. Skilled and stylish, she wore a bright purple satin flying suit.

One of the most famous barnstormers of the 1920s was Bessie Coleman. She was the first black woman to earn a pilot's license. It wasn't easy. Nobody in the United States would teach her to fly because she was female and black. So she trained in France. A fearless barnstormer, she was known as "Queen Bess, Daredevil Aviatrix." She thrilled audiences with hair-raising stunts. In one, she climbed high, then stalled her engine. The audience gasped as the plane plunged toward the ground. At the last minute, Bessie calmly restarted the engine and soared over the cheering crowd.

Many other women fliers have become famous, from Amelia Earhart and Beryl Markham to racing pilot Jackie Cochran. Today, women fly every kind of craft from jetliners to space shuttles, and have proven they are just as skilled as men.

Bessie Coleman
A great barnstormer, she was the fir[st] African American woman pilot.

Ruth Blaney Alexander
This American flier set a woman's altitude record of 26,000 feet in 193[ ]

Harriet Quimby
This pilot was the first American woman to earn a flying license. In 1912, she became the first woman to fly over the English Channel. She died in an accident when wind upset her plane, tipping her out.

Famous Firsts

Patty Wagstaff, first woman National Aerobatics champion, flies her Extra 260 (left). Below, astronaut Eileen Collins, first woman space shuttle pilot, makes log notes in the shuttle Columbia.

Women Service Pilots

During World War II, these women fliers served as Women's Airforce Service Pilots (WASPs). They delivered planes to combat zones, and flew everything from fighters to heavy bombers.

Traveling by Air

Meals in the Sky
A girl and her mother eat lunch, served by a stewardess on a 1941 Douglas DC-3 airliner. Hot meals, cushioned seats, and pressurized cabins made flights much more comfortable and enjoyable.

Do you remember your first airplane trip and how exciting it was to take off and fly over the clouds? Today, Boeing 747 and 777 jumbo jets carry 400 passengers on long nonstop flights over the ocean. People enjoy meals, nap, or watch movies. In just hours, they are whisked to their destinations. Yet the first airliner in 1914 was a tiny plane that carried one passenger. It flew between Tampa and St. Petersburg, Florida.

Some of the earliest airliners were converted World War I bomber planes. The engines were so noisy, passengers couldn't talk. They wrote notes to each other instead. In the 1920s and 30s, builders produced faster, safer, more reliable all-metal airliners. These larger planes carried more passengers, and soon stewardesses were hired to care for them.

The most luxurious airliners of the 1930s were giant flying boats. They had bottoms shaped like boat hulls and floats under their wings instead of wheels. People felt safe crossing the ocean in them because they could land on water. The biggest, Pan American's 314 , was like a flying luxury hotel. By the 1940s, airliners had air-conditioned, pressurized cabins for greater comfort. In the 1950s, the first passenger jetliners flew.

Flight Attendants

The first stewardesses, hired by United Airlines in 1930 (below) were registered nurses. Later flight attendants worked for many airlines and wore their wings and badges (left).

Built to Last

The most successful propeller-driven airliner ever made, the Douglas DC-3, first came into service in 1936. Over 13,000 of the planes were built. Today, more than 1,000 are still flown worldwide.

Flying Boat

The Boeing 314 Clipper, 106 feet long, took off and landed on water. It carried 74 passengers. In this model you can see inside: It had a dining room, galley, lounge, and even sleeping berths.

DELTA AIR LINES

I. R. JACKSON 408

BAGGAGE COMPARTMENT

WOMEN'S POWDER ROOM

FOURTH COMPARTMENT

SIXTH COMPARTMENT

SUITE DE LUXE

Flight Control

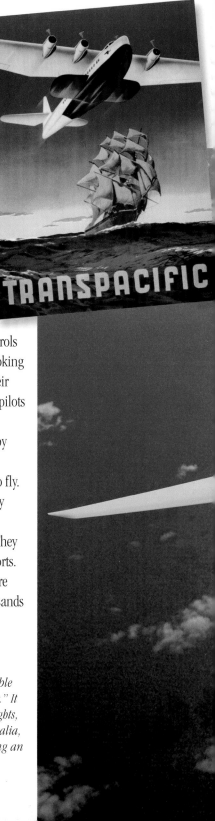

Flying and controlling an airplane today is very different than it was when the Wright brothers first flew in 1903. Modern planes are fast, complex machines that require great skill to operate. And so many people now travel by air that the skies are crowded with jets streaking to destinations worldwide.

The cockpit is an airplane's nerve center. It is chock-full of instruments, controls, and computer screens. A Boeing 747 cockpit has over 900 different controls and instrument dials. Where pilots once navigated by looking down on the ground for landmarks, they now look at their navigation screens. They also rely on computerized autopilots that control flight more accurately than a human can.

Air traffic controllers on the ground track planes by radar and guide them by radio. They keep planes from colliding in midair by telling each plane which path to fly. Today's pilots fly in special "air corridors," invisible sky highways marked on navigation maps.

Commercial airports were first built in the 1920s. They were tiny compared to today's enormous city airports. The world's busiest airport, Chicago's O'Hare Airport, is a bustling center where thousands of planes land and take off each day.

Cockpit View
In the cockpit of a DC-3 airliner (top), pilot and co-pilot sit side by side. Each has a set of instruments to control the plane. The DC-3 cruised at 230 miles an hour. Easy to fly, it was popular with pilots.

Early Airports
Airports of the 1940s, like the one shown here, had few buildings and runways compared to today's sprawling city airports.

Flight of the Future
Tomorrow's jetliners may resemble Boeing's planned "Sonic Cruiser." It would fly passengers on long flights, such as London to Sydney, Australia, at near supersonic speeds, cutting an hour off every 3,000 miles.

Flying the World

A 1930s travel brochure advertises Pan American's 314 Clipper, named after fast clipper ships. It flew over the ocean at 174 miles an hour. Now jets zoom round the globe at over 600 miles an hour.

Traffic Control

Inside an airport control tower, air traffic controllers monitor planes flying along many airways by radar. Bright dots on the radar screens show the position of each plane in its flight path.

To the Limits

Bell X-1

Test pilot Chuck Yeager stands with the rocket-powered Bell X-1 he test-flew, named Glamorous Glennis *for his wife. Today, it hangs in the National Air and Space Museum (below).*

Flying a plane to its limits is a test pilot's job. In 1947, test pilot Chuck Yeager prepared for a dangerous mission. He would try to fly a bright orange, bullet-shaped plane with a rocket engine faster than the speed of sound to break through the sound barrier. This was an invisible "wall" in the sky. Many pilots traveling at high speed had hit it. Their planes would shake and buck violently. Some even flew apart. Nearing the speed of sound, shock waves battered the planes. Many pilots died.

On October 14, 1947, Yeager flew the orange plane, the Bell X-1. To save fuel, it was carried up by a B-29 mother plane. Yeager climbed down into the X-1 cockpit and the craft was dropped into the sky. "My heart was in my mouth and my stomach right behind," he said. He fired the plane's rocket engine and the X-1 took off, pushing to over 700 miles an hour. This was past Mach 1, or the speed of sound. Inside, Yeager felt the plane rock violently. Suddenly, the Machmeter needle jumped, and the X-1 blasted through the barrier. The bumping stopped and Yeager flew on smoothly. He was the first person to fly faster than sound!

Other fliers have pushed their craft to see how far in distance they could go. In 1986, pilots Dick Rutan and Jeana Yeager flew a lightweight plane called the *Voyager*. They traveled nonstop around the world without refueling, setting a new record. In 1999, Swiss Pilot Bertrand Piccard and British pilot Brian Jones flew nonstop around the world by balloon. They traveled over mountains, deserts, and oceans in another record flight. Their balloon was the *Breitling Orbiter 3*.

Flying Fast

On October 14, 1947, this picture was taken of the Bell X-1 as its rockets fired and it shot off toward the sound barrier. Pilot Chuck Yeager became the first human to fly faster than sound.

Ballooning the World

Drifting over the snow-capped Alps, the Breitling Orbiter 3, *a silver-colored balloon filled with helium and hot air, travels around the world in 1999. It flew 30,000 miles in just under 20 days, setting a record.*

No Fuel Stops

In 1986, the Voyager, *a propeller plane, flies nonstop around the world. It flew 24,000 miles in 9 days. The light plane carried fuel even in its long thin wings. Today, the plane hangs in the Museum.*

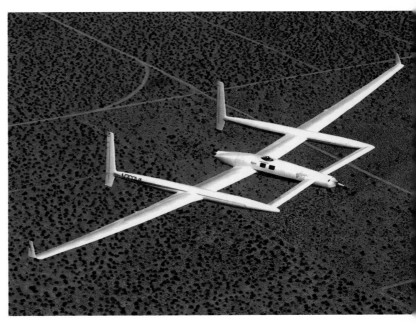

Blast Off!

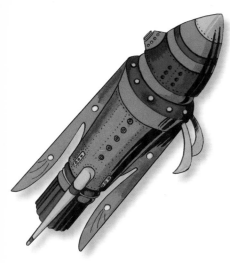

Comics Spaceship

In the 1930s, kids enjoyed the space adventures of cartoon hero Buck Rogers, who fought aliens and traveled in spaceships like this.

Rocket Scientist

In 1926, Dr. Robert Goddard launched the first liquid-fueled rocket from his aunt's farm in Massachusetts. It shot up 41 feet in 2 ½ seconds.

Rocket engines are the most powerful on Earth. The first rockets were invented by the Chinese. Back in the 1200s, Chinese soldiers were using weapons described as "arrows of flying fire." These were bamboo tubes attached to arrows. The user would light gunpowder in an open end to fire the rocket toward an enemy. The early Chinese also used rockets as fireworks, something we still do today.

By the 20th century, people had begun to think of using rockets to explore space. Rocket engines produce massive launching power. And they are the only engines that can work in space because they carry their own oxygen, called oxidizer. In space there is no air, so no oxygen. Most engines, like jet engines, need oxygen from the atmosphere to burn fuel and couldn't operate in space.

How does a rocket work? Very much like a balloon. When you blow up a balloon and release it…Whoosh! It's gone. Inside a rocket, when the rocket fuel mixes with the oxidizer, combustion takes place. This creates powerful hot gases that build up under pressure. When they escape from the end, or nozzle, of the rocket, the rocket takes off.

In 1961, Soviet cosmonaut Yuri Gagarin became the first human to travel in space, launched by a rocket. But by 1969, American Apollo 11 astronauts were on their way to the moon. They were launched into space by the biggest rocket ever built, the Saturn V. You can see it launching Apollo 11 at right. This rocket towered as high as a 40-story building. It used nearly 3,000 tons of rocket fuel and traveled at 6,000 miles an hour.

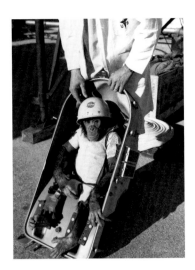

Beam Me Up

In 1961, Ham, a chimpanzee, rode a Mercury rocket 157 miles high. His safe return led to the flight of the first astronaut in space, Alan B. Shepard.

Awesome Engines

Workers inspect five huge engines of a Saturn V (left) that launched Apollo spacecraft. They produced power equal to that of 8 Hoover Dams.

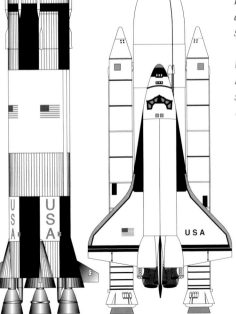

Out of Sight

Blasting a fiery trail, the space shuttle Columbia roars into the sky. Powered by two solid rocket boosters and its own engines, it will zoom to space in minutes.

Many Rockets

Rockets come in many different sizes. Here, you can compare three U.S. rockets. Left to right: Saturn V, the space shuttle, and Mercury Atlas.

Visions of the Moon

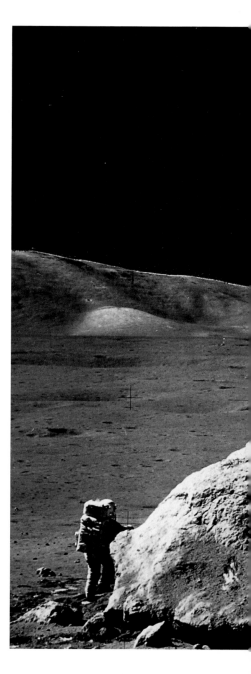

Since ancient times, people have been fascinated by the moon. Gazing up at the bright circle of light at night, many early people believed the moon was a powerful god or goddess. Some saw in it the features of a face—the Man in the Moon. Others saw a cat or beautiful woman. Some imagined the moon was made of green cheese. Still others feared it. According to one old superstition, sleeping in moonlight would make you go insane. This is where the word *lunatic* comes from. The Latin word for moon is *luna*.

Many early people imagined going to the moon and wondered what it was like. They dreamed of traveling in ships lifted by birds or balloons. In 1835, Englishman Richard Adams Locke made up a story. It claimed that a British astronomer had seen lush gardens and fantastic creatures on the moon through a huge new telescope. Pictures were published of these plants and creatures, but they were soon exposed as the "Great Moon Hoax."

Later, science fiction tales were written about imaginary visits to the moon. French author Jules Verne wrote two such books, *From the Earth to the Moon* in 1865 and *Around the Moon* in 1870. The reality of what the moon really looks like would not be discovered until nearly a century later.

Fly Me to the Moon

In this 1836 Italian illustration, a fanciful airship called the Diligence *rises on its way up to the moon. Lifted by one large and five small balloons, it has fins like bat wings for steering.*

Fantasy Vs. Reality

In this 1836 vision, men visit a moon garden with winged lunar women. The real moon landscape (below) proved quite different!

SCOPERTA LUNARE

Moon Creatures

Among many other fantastic moon beings imagined by an artist in 1836 were a flying "bat man," a one-horned moon bison similar to a unicorn, and a moon antelope.

Man on the Moon

Final Mission

Apollo 17 astronaut Eugene Cernan salutes the American flag he planted on the moon in 1972. This was the las[t] time humans visited the moon. A rod keeps the flag extended, since there is no lunar wind to make it flutter.

In 1969, after years of research and hard work, the fantastic dream of flying to the moon came true! On July 16, three U.S. astronauts climbed into a tiny spacecraft on top of the mighty Saturn V. It blasted off, lifting the craft up toward the moon. On July 19, Apollo 11 reached the moon. On July 20, two of the crew descended in the lander craft, the *Eagle*. Then, for the first time in history, human beings set foot on the moon. The first man, Neil Armstrong, said, "That's one small step for man, one giant leap for mankind." Then Buzz Aldrin got out. The men bounced in the moon's light gravity, collected lunar rocks, and planted an American flag. People on Earth watched through special TV cameras. Five more Apollo missions landed men on the moon. They drove a special car, the Lunar Rover, to explore the moon's mountains, plains, and craters. The first footsteps of Armstrong and Aldrin are still on the moon because there is no wind or rain to wash or blow them away.

Apollo 11 Crew

The astronauts of Apollo 11, first mission to land men on the moon, included from left: Neil Armstrong, commander, Michael Collins, and Edwin "Buzz" Aldrin, Jr. Above, Aldrin steps down onto the moon from the lander Eagle. *The mission patch (top) depicts the* Eagle's *landing.*

Splashdown

To come home, the astronauts reentered Earth's atmosphere in their spacecraft capsule and splashed down in the Pacific Ocean. Here, U.S. Navy divers come to pick them up.

Rocky Treasure

Astronauts used these tools to collect lunar rocks: a map book, sample box, and tongs. Below, lab workers on Earth study a large lunar rock. Such samples gave clues about the moon's past.

Space Suits

No one could survive in space for more than a few seconds without protection. There is no air to breathe and the air pressure is much too low for humans to endure. Temperatures in space can be extremely cold or hot. In the sun's glare, it may be a scorching 290° F. In the shade, it could be a frigid -264° F.

A space suit is like a mini spacecraft. It provides oxygen to breathe, protection from extreme heat or cold, a waste removal system, and a radio communication system so the astronauts can talk to each other. A space suit is made up of many layers. Some are tough outer layers to protect against small flying particles in space, called micrometeoroids. Other layers are soft, insulating fabrics that cushion and provide warmth. Underneath all this, astronauts wear a special underwear with a network of water-cooled tubing to keep the skin from overheating. It takes about 45 minutes just to get dressed in a space suit!

Going outside the spacecraft is called an EVA (extravehicular activity). In a space suit an astronaut can survive up to eight hours. The space suits are bulky, but not heavy in the weightlessness of space. They allow astronauts to do hard jobs, such as building parts of a space station. Earlier astronauts used a large jet-propelled backpack to move about freely in space. Today, astronauts stay tethered to the spacecraft by long cords for safety. They wear small jetpacks to return in case they accidentally get stranded.

Early Space Fashions

In the 1930s Buck Rogers cartoon (above), Buck and his girlfriend wore flexible metal space suits. In 1954, the hero of a movie The Rocket Man *(below) wore this suit, complete with a ray gun.*

High Altitude Suit

In 1935, American flier Wiley Post designed this pressure suit to fly safely at high altitudes. The suit resembled a deep-sea diver's outfit. A tube carried oxygen to the helmet. In this suit, Post flew to a record 55,000 feet high.

Mercury Astronauts

The seven Mercury astronauts were America's first men in space. They wore silver-colored space suits with an outer layer of reflective aluminized nylon. Getting into the suits required zipping 13 zippers.

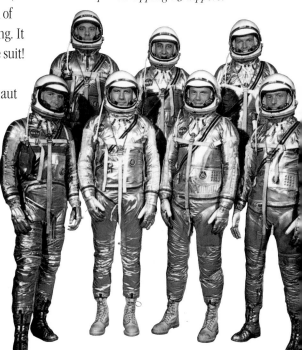

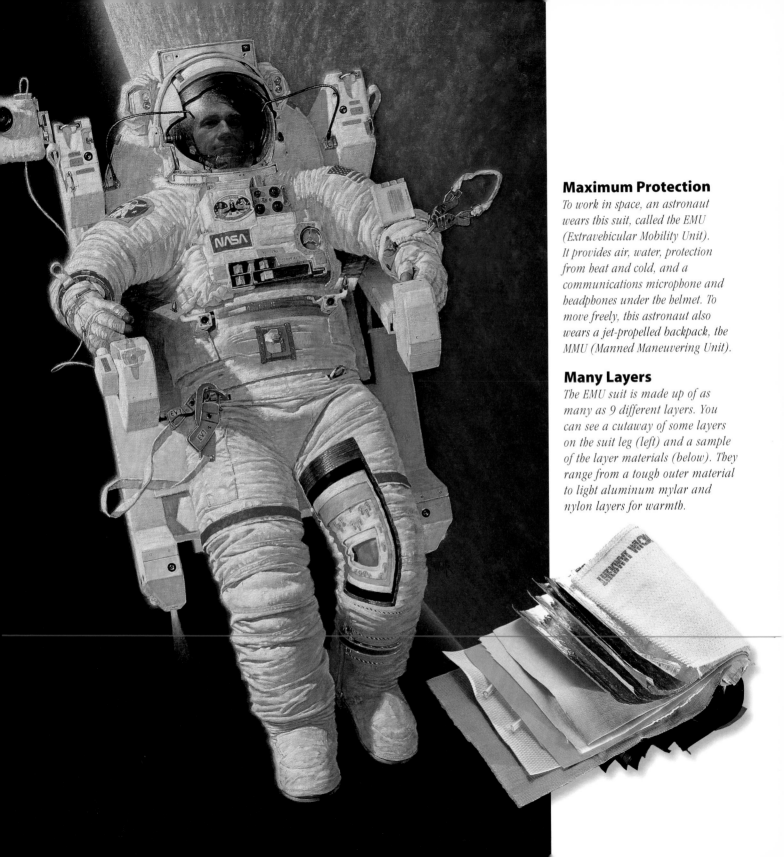

Maximum Protection

To work in space, an astronaut wears this suit, called the EMU (Extravehicular Mobility Unit). It provides air, water, protection from heat and cold, and a communications microphone and headphones under the helmet. To move freely, this astronaut also wears a jet-propelled backpack, the MMU (Manned Maneuvering Unit).

Many Layers

The EMU suit is made up of as many as 9 different layers. You can see a cutaway of some layers on the suit leg (left) and a sample of the layer materials (below). They range from a tough outer material to light aluminum mylar and nylon layers for warmth.

Shuttle Liftoff

On April 12, 1981, people at Kennedy Space Center in Florida watched the first space shuttle launch in history. " Three…two…one…zero. Liftoff!" The engines ignited, and *Columbia* blasted into the sky. Inside, astronauts Robert Crippen and John Young endured a jaw-shaking ride, then felt a calm as the craft climbed to space. "Smooth as silk," they reported.

Unlike earlier spacecraft, which could only be used once, the space shuttle was designed to be used over and over. The shuttle launches like a rocket with twin rocket boosters and a huge external tank of fuel. The airplane-like part of the shuttle is the orbiter. At liftoff, the orbiter's engines and two rocket boosters fire. Two minutes later, the boosters fall off. They parachute to the ocean, to be recovered and reused. The big fuel tank supplies fuel to the main engines, then falls off. It's the only part not reused. About eight minutes after launch, the shuttle reaches Earth orbit.

Out to Launch
The space shuttle Columbia *moves toward the launch pad at Kennedy Space Center in Florida. With its huge orange fuel tank and two rocket boosters, the shuttle weighs about 2,200 tons. It takes the world's biggest land vehicle, called the crawler, to carry it.*

Let's Go!
A space shuttle crew waves before leaving for launch. The crew includes a commander, pilot, and mission specialists trained for specific jobs, such as launching satellites or repairing telescopes.

Hot Stuff
Like a suit of armor, thermal tiles up to 5 inches thick cover the shuttle's nose and belly. They shield the craft so it won't burn up reentering Earth's atmosphere in searing heat of 3,000° F.

Mission Control

Mission Control, at Johnson Space Center in Houston, Texas, monitors every move of the space shuttle and crew. Experts there maintain contact with the shuttle as it orbits Earth with help from tracking stations worldwide.

What a Blast!

With a thundering roar, Columbia lifts off. The orbiter's engines, plus two solid rocket boosters, fire to push the craft into space. The huge orange tank, 15 stories high, holds 800 tons of liquid hydrogen and liquid oxygen to fuel the engines. It takes 7 million pounds of thrust, or force, to lift the shuttle into orbit.

At the Controls

The shuttle cockpit is located on the flight deck, the upper part of the orbiter cabin. In the picture here, the seats have been removed. The mission commander sits on the left and the pilot sits on the right, facing the front windows. The cockpit has more than 2,100 controls—dials, switches, indicator lights, and display screens. This is over a hundred times more controls than an average car has. Either the commander or the pilot can control the craft from his or her seat. Using the controls, they can fly the shuttle, operate a robot arm that lifts or retrieves objects outside the shuttle, or open and close the door of the payload bay, or cargo hold.

The space shuttle does not fly as far away from Earth as the Apollo spacecraft. It orbits at about 250 miles above Earth and travels at about 17,000 miles an hour. Many instruments help keep the craft on course. One is the star tracker. It constantly pinpoints the shuttle's position in relation to the stars. A complex computer system on board allows Mission Control in Houston, Texas, to operate the shuttle automatically. During flight, the commander or pilot can stay on automatic pilot, steer by control stick with computer assistance, or fly by direct control with no computer help.

Returning to Earth, the orbiter flies as a glider, with no power. The commander guides it in to land. He must aim carefully to land on the runway, because the craft cannot turn around and fly back to try again.

Gliding In

Wheels down, the shuttle Discovery comes in to land. A shuttle does not use its engines to land, but flies as a glider. It can land automatically, but the commander usually takes control to steer it to touchdown.

Glass Cockpit

A maze of controls, the shuttle cockpit has so many computer screens it's called the "glass cockpit." A single astronaut can operate the controls. They can also be operated by Mission Control.

Look's Good

Inside the shuttle Discovery, pilot Steven Lindsey (left) and mission specialist Stephen Robinson check a wire to be sure it's working properly. Shuttle controls are carefully monitored during flight.

Astro Bear

Dressed in a flight suit, "Magellan T. Bear," first teddy bear in space, flew on the shuttle Discovery *in 1995. He was sponsored by a group of school children.*

Working Out

In the weightlessness of space, muscles weaken. So humans exercise to stay healthy. On the International Space Station, Russian Yury Usachev peddles a cycle machine.

Living in Space

Astronauts in space do everything we do on Earth to live. They breathe, eat, sleep, use the bathroom, wash, and relax. The biggest difference between living on Earth and living in space is weightlessness. Inside the shuttle, there is so little gravity it's often called "zero gravity." Astronauts float about, hang upside down, even stand on the ceiling of the spacecraft. This takes getting used to. Most astronauts have nausea the first few days. Then they begin to enjoy it. How does it feel? Like going over a hill on a roller coaster—only better!

The shuttle crew live on the lower level of the cabin, called the mid-deck. It has a bathroom, small kitchen, or galley, and areas for sleeping, eating, and exercising. The cabin is heated and pressurized with normal air. The crew of two to seven wear comfortable light clothing. They eat three meals a day, and take turns preparing meals for the whole crew. Foods such as fruits are eaten fresh. Other foods are freeze-dried and mixed with water. Drinks must be sipped through a straw. If a drop of juice "escapes," it will simply float around. It must be captured to keep the cabin clean.

Astronauts don't take showers. They squirt water and soap into a towel or sponge and clean off. They use edible toothpaste they can swallow and dry shampoo. To sleep, astronauts curl up in a sleeping bag tied to a wall or sleep in a bunk bed. Before falling asleep, some enjoy looking out a window, watching the Earth go by below.

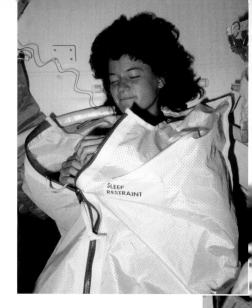

Catching Some ZZZs

Astronaut Sally Ride, first U.S. woman in space, takes a nap in the shuttle. She sleeps zipped up in a sleep restraint bag, attached to a wall so she won't drift away.

Space Toilet

The shuttle toilet in the small bathroom has foot restraints and hand bars so astronauts using it won't float away. It uses no water. Instead, a vacuum flush pulls waste into a tank.

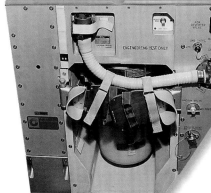

Mission Patch

Each space shuttle mission has its own patch, showing the names of the ship and crew and a picture of the mission job. This mission will use the shuttle's robot arm.

What's for Dinner?

In the galley, commander Tom Henricks takes his turn making the crew a meal. He pulls out dried foods to prepare and heat up in the oven. Favorite dishes include shrimp, tortillas, and chicken.

Look, Ma, No Hands!

Astronaut Carl Waltz floats through a tunnel on the shuttle. In zero gravity, everything floats freely, including people. You can glide or somersault with ease. Astronauts say it feels great.

Heat and Eat

This packet contains broccoli and cheese. To serve, you stick in a needle, inject hot water, and heat. To eat, you take scissors, snip an opening for a spoon, and dig in.

Working in Space

In space, astronauts spend a typical day working inside or outside the spacecraft. Inside jobs could include doing scientific experiments to test chemicals, grow crystals, or study the effects of weightlessness on the human body. Other jobs might be studying the Earth or stars and taking photographs. Sometimes astronauts spend their time inside just cleaning the spacecraft.

When they go outside to work, the astronauts put on their space suits and pass through an airlock to the payload bay. There, they may use the shuttle's robot arm, the Remote Manipulator System, to put a new satellite into orbit or bring one in for repair. Sometimes, the astronauts work in Spacelab, a small laboratory that is pressurized and carried in the cargo bay. Astronauts can work on scientific experiments there without wearing space suits. Spacelab can hold many kinds of scientific instruments, including telescopes to study the universe.

Smile, Earth

Cosmonaut Yuri Gidzenko takes a photograph of Earth from the International Space Station. Crews in space take many pictures of Earth to help scientists study our planet's ecological health.

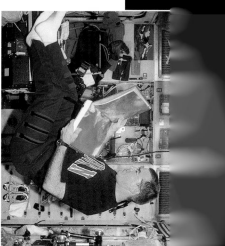

Mapping It Out

On the space station, astronaut James Voss studies an atlas. He will pinpoint an area on Earth the crew has been assigned to look at from space.

Studying Volcanoes

Smoke and ash billow from a volcano in this photograph taken from the shuttle. Such images help experts monitor the ash cloud to warn people in its way and predict future eruptions.

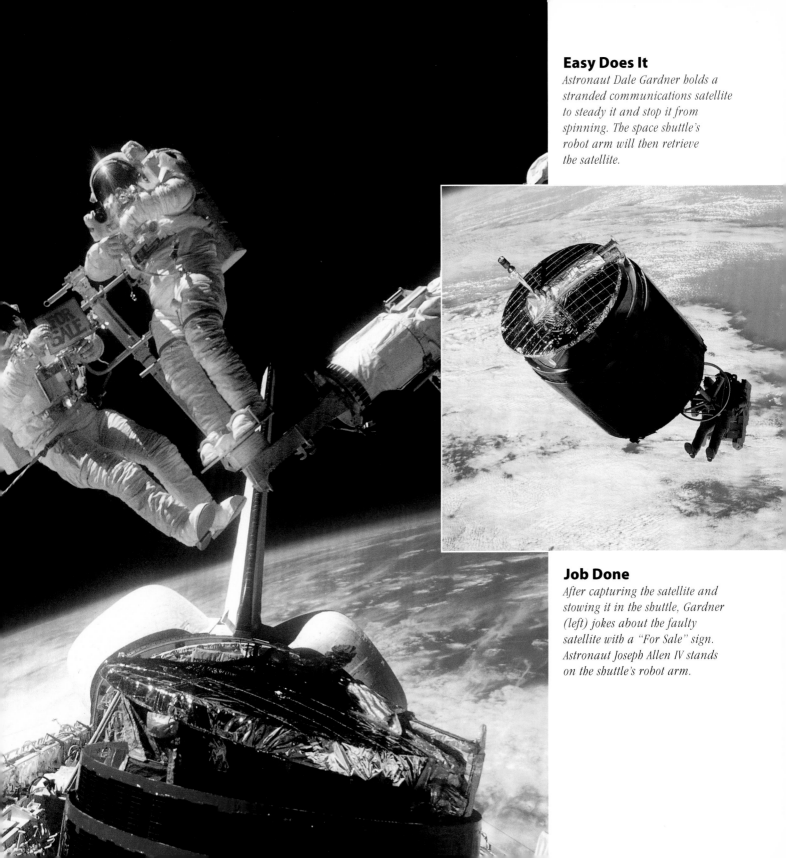

Easy Does It

Astronaut Dale Gardner holds a stranded communications satellite to steady it and stop it from spinning. The space shuttle's robot arm will then retrieve the satellite.

Job Done

After capturing the satellite and stowing it in the shuttle, Gardner (left) jokes about the faulty satellite with a "For Sale" sign. Astronaut Joseph Allen IV stands on the shuttle's robot arm.

The Space Station

Space Cities

The idea of a space station is not new. For years, science-fiction tales, like ones in this 1953 magazine, described people building and living in fantastic cities far beyond the Earth.

Someday you may be lucky enough to visit or work on a space station. The new International Space Station (ISS) today orbits high over the Earth. The largest object ever built in space, it circles the Earth 16 times a day, traveling over 17,000 miles an hour. The ISS is a joint project of 16 different nations, including the United States, Canada, Russia, countries of the European Space Agency, and Japan. It was started in 1998 and is still being built. It replaces an older Russian space station, called *Mir*.

New parts for the space station must be ferried up from Earth by the space shuttle or other spacecraft. On the station, a large robot arm contributed by Canada helps assemble the new parts. The station is scheduled to be finished sometime around 2006.

Today, the ISS is home to an international crew. Now about as tall as a 14-story building, the ISS has giant winglike solar panels that provide electricity. The crew live in spacious quarters with a kitchen, dining area, bathroom, and places to sleep, exercise, and relax. The station already has the first of several planned scientific laboratories. There, crew do research to learn more about space and test new medicines to help fight diseases, such as cancer and AIDS. Because people can live many months on a space station, they can also study the long-term effects of life in space. In the future, the ISS may be a launch site for new space missions to the moon and to Mars.

Wheel Colony

This image of a space station shaped like a wheel appeared in a 1950s Walt Disney movie Man and the Moon. *Here, the station is being built piece by piece by workers in spacecraft.*

Out of This World

Orbiting 220 miles over Earth, the International Space Station is today home to a crew of 3. When complete, it will stretch over an area the size of two football fields and weigh a million pounds. This photograph, taken from a space shuttle, shows the station's new Canadian robot arm.

Looking at Space

Look at the astronauts in the picture at right. Can you imagine working hundreds of miles above the Earth, standing on the end of a long moving pole? Some people call it the world's highest diving board. Of course, it's really the robot arm of the space shuttle. And this picture shows it doing one of its most important jobs.

In 1993, a crew from the shuttle *Endeavour* traveled up to space after training for a year. They had prepared for a special repair job. They would work on the new Hubble Space Telescope, a silver-colored cylinder about the size of a school bus. It had been put in orbit outside Earth's atmosphere. It was expected to make much clearer pictures of the universe, since the clouds and atmosphere distort views from telescopes on Earth. Unfortunately, the first pictures from the new space telescope were blurry because of a faulty mirror system.

The *Endeavour* crew expertly replaced the mirror equipment and added a new camera. When the new telescope pictures came in, they were clear and fantastic! They opened up a whole new window on the universe. With the space telescope, it is now possible to see objects in our solar system in much greater detail. We can also see some distant stars and galaxies that were never visible before.

High-Rise Repair

In 1993, two astronauts of the shuttle Endeavour *repair the Hubble Space Telescope. They stand on the shuttle's robot arm, attached to the payload bay, high above Earth.*

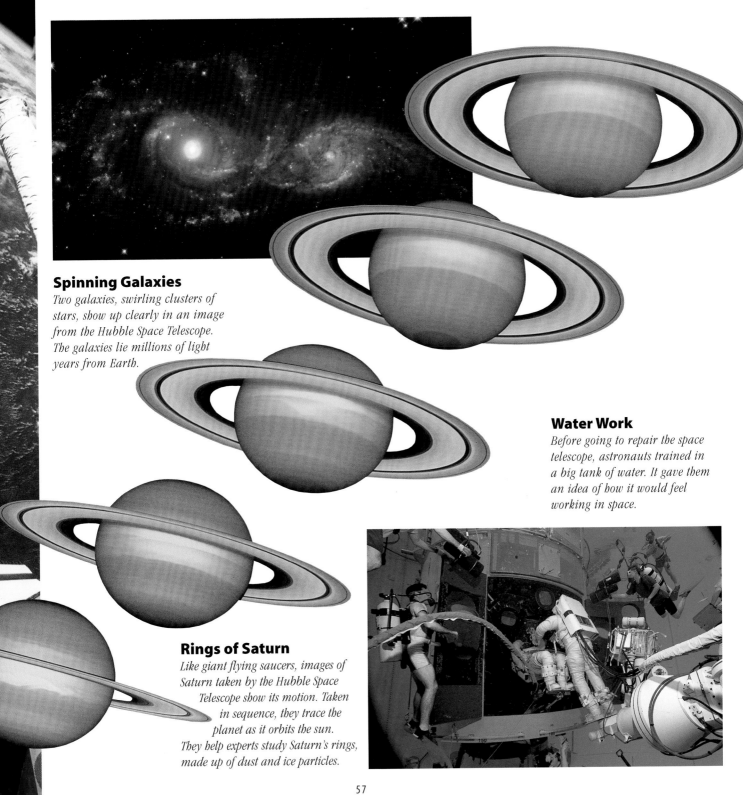

Spinning Galaxies

Two galaxies, swirling clusters of stars, show up clearly in an image from the Hubble Space Telescope. The galaxies lie millions of light years from Earth.

Water Work

Before going to repair the space telescope, astronauts trained in a big tank of water. It gave them an idea of how it would feel working in space.

Rings of Saturn

Like giant flying saucers, images of Saturn taken by the Hubble Space Telescope show its motion. Taken in sequence, they trace the planet as it orbits the sun. They help experts study Saturn's rings, made up of dust and ice particles.

Bringing It Home

When it's time to come home, the shuttle pilot turns the ship toward Earth. He fires maneuvering rockets to drop out of orbit. The craft must leave orbit at exactly the right time and place to be able to land in the correct spot on Earth. The crew are strapped in their seats. Hurtling along at 25 times the speed of sound, the orbiter reenters Earth's atmosphere. It's a bumpy ride. Tremendous friction from reentry jolts and shakes the craft and causes fiery heat that blasts around it like a furnace. The shuttle's tile heat shield works well to protect the ship so it doesn't burn up.

As the orbiter comes down to land, its power is off. It glides quietly. Pulled in by gravity, it moves back and forth in big S-shaped turns to slow down. Its speed gradually drops from 17,000 miles an hour to 350 miles an hour. At about 20 miles from the runway, the commander guides the orbiter in to land. It touches down like an airplane. The astronauts get off by walking down landing steps.

Today, there are four space shuttles operating. They are the *Columbia*, *Atlantis*, *Discovery*, and *Endeavour*. Another shuttle, the *Challenger*, blew up shortly after launch in a terrible accident in 1986. Altogether, the shuttles have flown over 100 missions.

Hitching a Ride

After landing in California, the shuttle Columbia *rides piggyback on a Boeing 747. With no power to fly after landing, it must be ferried back to Kennedy Space Center in Florida.*

Touchdown

As the shuttle orbiter hits the runway at about 200 miles an hour, a drag chute, or tail parachute, opens. It helps slow the craft down so it can gradually brake to a stop.

Inside View

Here, you can see inside the shuttle Discovery. *The payload bay doors are open and the robot arm holds a satellite. The crew cabin and flight deck are located at the front of the 120-foot-long orbiter.*

Into the Future

Today, scientists and designers are busy planning tomorrow's space travel. What will future space vehicles look like? Check out the designs on these pages. They're all artist's visions of new or recent ideas.

The space shuttle is very expensive to operate. Launching it requires huge amounts of rocket fuel. Inventors now hope to create a new generation of space planes that can reach orbit without the costly launch system of the shuttle. Some new planes might even take off, orbit, and land all in one unit. This would be much cheaper and more convenient than the shuttle.

To make things more interesting, inventors can now compete in a new contest. It's called the X Prize Competition. Just as cash prizes inspired early aviators like Charles Lindbergh to try new challenges, the X-Prize will inspire inventors today. It will award $10 million for the best new privately designed manned space vehicle to reach an altitude of 62 miles. So far, inventors from several countries have submitted ideas. You can see some here.

VentureStar
Blasting a fiery trail, this space plane, called the X-33 or VentureStar, was an earlier idea for a totally reusable vehicle. It would take off like a rocket, orbit, and land like an airplane.

Hyper-X
Designed by NASA, this research plane is called the X-43, or Hyper-X. It would fly at "hypersonic" speed, many times the speed of sound, to launch spacecraft into orbit.

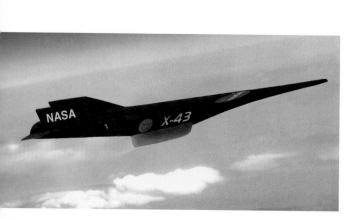

X Prize Designs

Three designs competing for the X Prize for new space vehicles include (1) The U.S. TGV Rockets suborbital craft (left). This rocket-powered ship slows its landing by opening an umbrella-like drag skirt; (2) The British Ascender space plane (above) uses both jet and rocket engines to reach space; (3) The Russian Cosmopolis XXI (below) would ride piggyback up on a jet carrier, then fly vertically up to space.

Journey to Mars

Imagine traveling on a spacecraft bound for Mars. Scientists believe it is possible to send a manned mission to explore Mars within two decades. What might you find on Mars, our neighbor in the solar system? For one thing, you would discover it's red because of reddish iron oxide in its soil. Mars is also bitterly cold. And it has some features like ours on Earth, including polar ice caps and mountains. It also has a volcano three times as tall as Mount Everest!

For years people have wondered if life exists on Mars. In 1896, British author H.G. Wells wrote a science-fiction book *The War of the Worlds*. It described scary Martians with tentacles who tried to conquer Earth. Later, people feared Martian "little green men." Since 1976, many robot probes have traveled to Mars, including the 1976 Viking landers, 1997 Pathfinder, and 2001 Mars Odyssey. From these craft, we know that Mars is a rocky desert today. Yet experts believe it once had water and maybe microscopic life. A mission to Mars would take months, even years. Explorers there might discover hidden sources of water. And they, or robotic spacecraft, might finally learn if other life has existed in the universe. Like the trip to the moon, human exploration of Mars may one day be a reality. Perhaps you will be part of that exciting journey!

Martian Attack!
Spewing fire, Martians in flying saucers attack Earth in the 1953 movie The War of the Worlds *(top). In 1938, a radio broadcast of the story on Halloween night terrified people, who believed it was true.*

New Robot Rover
In 2003, NASA will launch this Mars rover (above, left). It will travel over the red planet to study its climate history and search for signs where water and life may have once existed.

Destination Mars
Sometime in the next 20 years, humans may explore Mars. In this imaginary scene, two explorers from Earth stop their vehicle to inspect robot lander craft sent from Earth years earlier.

Fossil Clues

Did life ever exist on Mars? The best evidence may lie in fossils. Here, a mission specialist in geology studies a rock she picked up on Mars to look for traces of fossil life..

Index

Picture Credits